A YEAR OF

Greetings

VOLUME ONE

PAPER ADVENTURES®

WITH

Sally Traidman

A Year Of Greetings, Volume One
Copyright 2000 Paper Adventures

ISBN 0-9677364-1-2

Writers Sally Traidman, Mary Wohlgemuth
Editors Shanna dela Cruz, David Wilke
Art Director Shanna dela Cruz
Book Design Darla Farrant
Electronic Production Caryn Clark
Photography Alan Knox Photography
Photo Stylist Trisha Dallman
Pattern Creation Alpha Omega Graphics Inc.

Published in the United States by Paper Adventures
PO Box 04393 Milwaukee, WI 53204
Phone: 414-383-0414 Fax: 414-383-0760

Visit us at www.paperadventures.com

Manufactured in the United States of America

CONTENTS

A YEAR OF
Greetings
VOLUME ONE

INTRODUCTION

Each year brings many things: new faces, new celebrations, new memories. It also brings new opportunities to make especial events even more meaningful with a new handmade card and invitation idea starter book from Paper Adventures—A YEAR OF GREETINGS, VOLUME ONE.

A Year of Greetings, Volume One, offers 12 unique projects designed to help you mark special events with beautifully crafted, handmade greeting cards and invitations. There is one project for each month of the year—each one more creative, fun, and beautiful than the last. And like treasured notes, cards and letters from your past, this fun-filled idea book is sure to be a keepsake you will turn to time and time again for inspiration and direction.

We developed this book after many requests for a Paper Adventures idea book. As our goal, we strove to create a project book unlike any other. We wanted to create a yearbook line we could expand upon—year after year—that would continue to supply creative inspiration for card artists at every level. With that in mind we were thrilled to partner with Sally Traidman as our first Greetings Yearbook featured artist. Please read more about Sally in The Artist. It was a joy working with Sally. Her love of paper crafting shines through each page of this book.

THE ARTIST

Sally Traidman

"Card creation is fun. You don't have to be an artist or have a million stamps to create something beautiful, hand-crafted, and meaningful," says Sally Traidman, 18-year stamper and card creation veteran. "All you need is good paper, time, and the desire to create something special. Card creation makes you feel good. When you're done with a project you know that you have just created something original with your own two hands."

What makes stamping even more special is that each card is made with one person in mind, using their likes and dislikes as a guide. "It is a soothing craft. With stamps, papers, and accessories, you create rewarding, special things—unique gifts that mean so much more than a store-bought card. Recipients of a hand-made card know that you took the time, not only to remember them and their special event or occasion, but to care enough to give a part of yourself as well. That makes hand-made cards special."

Sally also feels that in today's hectic, automated, computer-driven lifestyle, taking time out to feed your creative soul, to find inspiration in life, is something that can not be underrated. "Stamping takes time, but it gives so much back. For example, this past summer when my eldest son was married, we created the invitations, response cards, programs—everything—by hand. It was time-consuming, but the resulting original cards were more than momentos, they will become cherished family heirlooms for a new generation. That is the power of card creation."

When asked what she found unique about this collection of designs, Sally said that the projects contained in this book have a very original feel. "They are unabashedly cheery. The paper and patterns give this collection a striking contemporary feel while being versatile and fun."

Sally Traidman has been designing cards for more than 18 years. Before turning to card creation and stamping she was an art teacher. Sally has led numerous classes, seminars, and workshops in stamping and is a regular at industry tradeshows. Sally currently lives in Grand Rapids, Michigan, with her husband, her youngest son, and her fluffy white dog. She enjoys traveling and owns her own stamp catalog business, The Rubber Stampler. (www.rubberstampler.com).

PAPER ADVENTURES

In 1901 an adventurous craftsman had a goal to manufacture the highest quality products from premium papers. His dedication and drive quickly brought him to the forefront of the paper industry. The business became a family tradition and today, the fourth and fifth generation of craftsmen and women continue to strive toward this goal with Paper Adventures, manufacturer of creative paper products and ideas to dazzle the imaginations of paper crafters worldwide.

Paper Adventures products are exclusively available through specialty scrapbook, rubber stamp and craft retailers. To find a Paper Adventures Authorized Retailer near you, please visit our website at www.paperadventures.com or contact our customer service team at 800-727-0699.

January

"HAPPY NEW YEAR"

Celebrate the New Year with a personal touch.

January

MATERIALS CHECKLIST

PAPER:

- ☐ Mix 'n' Match Archivals
  - Ivory
- ☐ Mix 'n' Match Metallic
  - Gold Nugget
- ☐ Parchlucent
  - Twilight
- ☐ Envelopes
  - A-2 (4 ³/₈" x 5 ³/₄")

TOOLS:

- ☐ Edge Accents Scissors
  - Deckle
- ☐ Heat tool
- ☐ Ruler
- ☐ Scissors, straight edge
- ☐ Scorer/Burnisher, natural bone

SUPPLIES:

- ☐ Archival Glue
- ☐ Embossing pad
- ☐ Embossing pen
- ☐ Embossing powder, gold
- ☐ Marker, gold metallic

STAMPS: (from Hero Arts)

- ☐ "Fireworks" (G1470)
- ☐ "Star Word Print" (S1714)
- ☐ "Star Spiral" (E1422)

HOW-TO INSTRUCTIONS

FOLDING CARD

Base Start by making a folding card from a sheet of 8 ½" x 11" Ivory. Cut in half to 8 ½" x 5 ½" and score with scorer/burnisher and fold in half to a folded size of 5 ½" x 4 ¼". Stamp "Bursting Fireworks" with embossing ink randomly over Ivory note folding card. Stamp "Star Word Print" in empty spaces, cover with gold embossing powder and emboss.

Layers Cut one square size 3" x 3" and one rectangle size 1 ⅝" x 4 ½" from Twilight Parchlucent. Lightly dab embossing pad over square piece. Sprinkle lightly with gold powder, shake off excess and emboss . Write "Happy New Year" on rectangle piece with embossing pen, cover with gold embossing powder and emboss. Use glue lightly to mount and layer papers as shown.

ANNOUNCEMENT

Base Using the Deckle Edge Accents scissors cut Gold Nugget paper to 5 ½" x 4 ½".

Layers Emboss shooting star on Ivory paper in gold. Trim with Deckle Edge Accents scissors and outline deckle edges with gold metallic marker. Cut a thin strip size ⅞" x 3 ⅝" from Ivory. Write "Happy New Year" with embossing pen and emboss in gold. Cut a 4 ½" x 3 ¼" rectangle piece of Twilight Parchlucent paper. Stamp and emboss small stars all over Twilight overlay and lightly glue on top of Gold Nugget card leaving a ½" border

Star Tail Take a small piece of Twilight Parchlucent and dab lightly with embossing pad, sprinkle with gold embossing powder and emboss. Cut ultra thin strips making a long fringe and mount under star. Mount star on Twilight rectangle with foam mounts. Attach Happy New Year strip with glue.

Create a folding card option for this project by mounting it on 8 ½" x 5 ½" scored card stock.

Tip

When you glue Parchlucent, try to place glue in areas that will be covered by other paper or may be obscured by a stamped image. If you cannot, then apply only the amount of glue that is absolutely necessary and press very lightly as the glue adheres.

(Place A here)

(A)

Cut using Edge Accents
Deckle Scissors

February

"VALENTINES"

Show your
Valentines how
special they are with
lovely handmade cards.

February

MATERIALS CHECKLIST

PAPER:

- [ ] Embossed Archivals
  - Rose Heartstrings
- [ ] Mix 'n' Match Archivals
  - Rose Hearts
  - Rose Polkadots
  - Rose Solid
  - Sugar Solid
- [ ] Mix 'n' Match Metallic
  - Gold Nugget
- [ ] Envelopes
  - A-2 (4 ³/₈" x 5 ³/₄")
  - Square (6 ¹/₂" x 6 ¹/₂")

TOOLS:

- [ ] Edge Accents Scissors
  - Scallop
- [ ] Heat Tool

- [ ] Hole Punch, ¹/₁₆"
- [ ] Ruler
- [ ] Scissors, straight edge
- [ ] Scorer/Burnisher, natural bone

SUPPLIES:

- [ ] Archival Glue
- [ ] Embossing pad
- [ ] Embossing powder, gold
- [ ] Foam mounts
- [ ] Ribbon, metallic gold mesh
- [ ] Wire, gold

STAMPS: (from Hero Arts)

- [ ] "Hearts by Design" (LL448)
- [ ] "Swirl Heart" (E1352)

HOW-TO INSTRUCTIONS

ANNOUNCEMENT

Base
Start by making a square folding card using a sheet of 8 $\frac{1}{2}$" x 11" Rose Hearts. Cut down to 5 $\frac{1}{2}$" wide x 11" tall with the hearts in the paper running horizontal. Score in half on 11" dimension with scorer/burnisher and fold. Cut a 4" square from Rose Embossed paper, center and glue to the folding card.

Heart
Gold emboss heart on Sugar paper and cut out with a Scallop Edge Accents scissors leaving about an $\frac{1}{8}$" border. Punch or use your straight edge scissors tip to create a tiny hole at the top of the embossed heart. Attach gold ribbon to heart with wire through hole. Attach heart, with ribbon in place, centered on Rose Embossed square with foam mounts.

FOLDING CARD

Base
Start by making a folding card from a sheet of 8 $\frac{1}{2}$" x 11" Rose Embossed Heartstrings. Cut in half to 8 $\frac{1}{2}$" x 5 $\frac{1}{2}$", score with scorer/burnisher and fold in half to a folded size of 5 $\frac{1}{2}$" x 4 $\frac{1}{4}$". Cut a 4" x $\frac{1}{2}$" strip of Gold Nugget paper. Mount strip on embossed folding card.

Hearts
Using heart stamps gold emboss four different patterned hearts on Rose Solid, Rose Hearts, Gold Nugget and Rose Polkadots as shown. Cut out hearts leaving a slight edge around the stamped images. Mount hearts randomly on gold strip with foam mounts. Cut a piece of Sugar Solid to 5 $\frac{1}{2}$" x 4 $\frac{1}{4}$" and glue inside folding card to create a writing area.

Tip
Using the same papers and techiques in these projects, try making your own recipe cards to send Valentine cookie recipes, or add your favorite Valentine cookie recipe to the inside of your cards.

February
PATTERNS

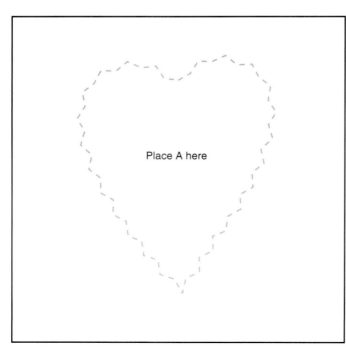

Place A here

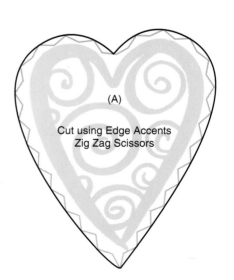

(A)

Cut using Edge Accents
Zig Zag Scissors

March

"BOUQUET"

Bring spring into the lives of friends and family a little early this year.

March

MATERIALS CHECKLIST

PAPER:

- [ ] Mix 'n' Match Archivals
  - Lime Polkadots
  - Strawberry Cream Polkadots
  - Sugar Solid
- [ ] Parchlucent
  - Crystal
- [ ] Parchlucent Prints
  - Strawberry Cream Polkadots
- [ ] Envelopes
  - A-2 (4 3/8" x 5 3/4")

TOOLS:

- [ ] Heat tool
- [ ] Hole punch 1/16"
- [ ] Ruler
- [ ] Scissors, straight edge
- [ ] Scorer/Burnisher, natural bone

SUPPLIES:

- [ ] Archival Glue
- [ ] Embossing pad
- [ ] Embossing powder, silver
- [ ] Markers
- [ ] Mix 'n' Match Raffia
  - Strawberry Cream, pearlized
- [ ] Paper fasteners, metallic miniature

STAMPS: (from Hero Arts)

- [ ] "Flowers in Vase" (H1460)

HOW-TO INSTRUCTIONS

FOLDING CARD I

Base Start by making a folding card from a sheet of 8 ¹/₂" x 11" Sugar Solid. Cut in half to 8 ¹/₂" x 5 ¹/₂" and fold in half to 5 ¹/₂" x 4 ¹/₂". Cut two Strawberry Cream and two Lime Polkadots 2" x 2 ¹/₂" rectangles. Arrange as pictured and glue onto Sugar folding card.

Flower & Vase Emboss flowers and vase in silver onto Strawberry Cream Parchlucent Prints Polkadots 3 ¹/₄" x 4 ¹/₂" rectangle. Color flowers and leaves with markers from the back of paper. Cut a piece of Sugar Solid paper 3 ¹/₂" x 4 ³/₄" to center under embossed Parchlucent Print then punch two holes through both layers according to pattern. Secure both layers together with Strawberry Cream raffia threaded through the holes and tied into a bow. Glue final layered piece with bow onto the Lime and Strawberry Cream Polkadots base as shown.

FOLDING CARD II

Base Start by making a Lime Polkadots folding card from an 8 ¹/₂" x 11". Cut in half to 8 ¹/₂" x 5 ¹/₂" and score with scorer/burnisher and fold in half to a folded size of 5 ¹/₂" x 4 ¹/₄". Cut 3 ³/₄" x 5" piece of Strawberry Cream Polkadots and glue, centered on Lime Polkadots folding card.

Flower & Vase Cut a Crystal Parchlucent rectangle smaller 3 ¹/₄" x 4 ¹/₂" and emboss flowers and vase in silver. Color flowers and leaves with markers from the back of paper. Tie tiny Strawberry Cream raffia knots and glue over embossed flowers. Attach embossed Parchlucent over-lay to Strawberry Cream Polkadots with miniature paper fasteners then mount to Lime folding card.

Tip

Coloring on the back of parchlucent produces a look almost like stained glass. It's perfect for when you want softened or muted colors. On Crystal Parchlucent the color becomes more pastel. It works well with markers or colored pencils.

When heat embossing on Parchlucent, use as little heat as necessary. Too much for too long can cause the paper to curl. Use just enought to solidify the embossing powder.

March

PATTERNS

Arrange and glue
Polkadot Square pieces
in this way

MATERIALS CHECKLIST

PAPER:

- ☐ Diamond Dust
  - Daffodil
  - Lime
  - Strawberry Cream
  - Wedgwood
- ☐ Mix 'n' Match Archivals
  - Celery Gingham
  - Celery Solid
  - Daffodil Solid
  - Grape Solid
  - Lilac Checkered
  - Lilac Polkadots
  - Lilac Solid
  - Lime Gingham
  - Lime Polkadots
  - Strawberry Cream Polkadots
  - Strawberry Cream Solid

- ☐ Mix 'n' Match Metallics
  - Gold Nugget
- ☐ Parchlucent
  - Crystal/Opal
- ☐ Envelopes
  - A-2 (4 ³/₈" x 5 ³/₄")
  - A-7 (5 ¹/₄" x 7 ¹/₄")

TOOLS:

- ☐ Edge Accents Scissors
  - Deckle
  - Scallop
- ☐ Heat tool
- ☐ Hole punch, ¹/₁₆"
- ☐ Knife, Craft/Hobby
- ☐ Ruler
- ☐ Scissors, straight edge
- ☐ Scorer/Burnisher, natural bone

SUPPLIES:

- ☐ Archival Glue
- ☐ Embossing pad
- ☐ Embossing powder
  - Clear
  - Gold
- ☐ Pigment pad, purple
- ☐ Mix 'n' Match Raffia
  - Lilac, pearlized
- ☐ Mix 'n' Match Ribbon
  - Lilac

STAMPS: (from Hero Arts)

- ☐ "Happy Easter" (F334)
- ☐ "Dainty Flower Background" (S18

HOW-TO INSTRUCTIONS

FOLDING CARD I

Base   Create a base size 4 ⁷/₈" x 6 ³/₄"" from Lilac Checkered Mix 'n' Match Archivals paper. Cut Crystal/Opal Parchlucent to fit on Lilac Checkered paper leaving about ¹/₁₆" border. Emboss "Happy Easter" on Parchlucent with purple pigment ink and clear embossing powder.

Basket & Eggs   Cut Daffodil Solid basket using the pattern. Using a craft knife and following the pattern cut vertical slits into basket. Weave thin paper strips cut from Lilac, Strawberry Cream and Celery Solid papers in an out of slits to make a woven basket. Use the pattern to cut eggs from Mix 'n' Match Archivals, Strawberry Cream Polkadots, Lilac Polkadots, Celery Gingham, and Daffodil Diamond Dust and Gold Nugget papers. Emboss Gold Nugget egg with floral patterned stamp. Arrange eggs and glue in basket as shown. Mount the basket on the Crystal/Opal Parchlucent overlay. Secure the assembled overlay onto the Lilac Checkered base by centering the Crystal/Opal Parchlucent and punching two mini holes in the corners through both layers. With tiny strip of Lilac raffia attach the Parchlucent with the basket to the Lilac Checkered folding card base. Tie a bow with the Lilac ribbon and adhere to basket with foam mounts.

FOLDING CARD II

Base   Start by making a folding card from a sheet of 8 ¹/₂" x 11" Grape Mix 'n' Match Archivals. Cut in half to 8 ¹/₂" x 5 ¹/₂" and score with scorer/burnisher and fold in half to a folded size of 5 ¹/₂" x 4 ¹/₄". Gold emboss "Happy Easter" on Grape paper folding card base. Cut a thin strip from Mix 'n' Match Metallics Gold Nugget paper the width of the folding card and glue about ¹/₂" from bottom.

Eggs   Cut eggs from Mix 'n' Match Archivals Strawberry Cream Polkadots, Lime Polkadots, Lilac Solid and Daffodil Solid and Diamond Dust Daffodil and Wedgwood using the pattern. Cut egg decorations using Scallop and Deckle Edge Accents scissors in a variety of papers and glue onto eggs. Mount decorated eggs randomly overlapping each other and Gold Nugget strip as shown. Cut small pieces of Lilac raffia in 1" lengths and fold in half. Glue folded pieces of Lilac raffia on for grass.

Tip

To easily make striped egg decorations line up with the shape of the base eggs cut out the egg shape in all the colors you plan to use for decoration. With Mammoth Edge Accents or Edge Accent scissors cut stripes from the eggs. Use those trimmed decorations to overlay and match exactly to the base egg.

April
PATTERNS

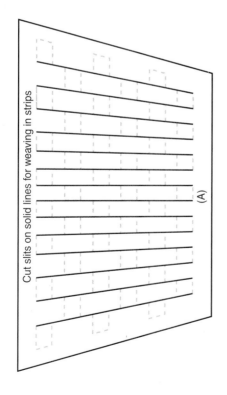

Cut slits on solid lines for weaving in strips

(A)

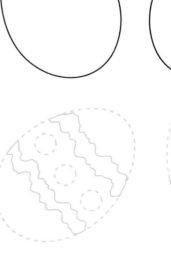

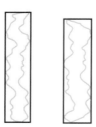

Cut using Edge Accents
Deckle Scissors

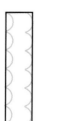

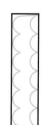

Cut using Edge Accents
Scallop Scissors

May

"BUTTERFLIES"

Butterfly
Bed and
Breakfast

To Cheer You

Butterflies adorn these colorful cards giving them an extra air of spring-into-summer cheer.

May

MATERIALS CHECKLIST

PAPER:

- ☐ Mix 'n' Match Archivals
  - Celery Solid
  - Daffodil Solid
  - Grape Polkadots
  - Grape Solid
  - Lilac Gingham
  - Lilac Polkadots
  - Lilac Solid
  - Strawberry Cream Solid
- ☐ Envelopes
  - A-2 (4 ³/₈" x 5 ³/₄")

TOOLS:

- ☐ Heat tool
- ☐ Hole punch, 1/4"
- ☐ Ruler
- ☐ Scissors, straight edge
- ☐ Scorer/Burnisher, natural bone

SUPPLIES:

- ☐ Archival Glue
- ☐ Embossing pad
- ☐ Embossing powder, gold
- ☐ Mix 'n' Match Raffia
  - Lilac

STAMPS: (from Hero Arts)

- ☐ "Butterfly" (A1489)
- ☐ "Butterfly" (E1483)
- ☐ "To Cheer You" (D1309)
- ☐ "Florentine" (S1838)

HOW-TO INSTRUCTIONS

FOLDING CARD

Base
Start by making a folding card from a sheet of 8 ½" x 11" Lilac Solid Mix 'n' Match. Cut in half to 8 ½" x 5 ½". Then score with scorer/burnisher and fold in half to a folded size of 5 ½" x 4 ½". Gold emboss "To Cheer You" greeting on the bottom of Lilac folding card.

Tag
Cut Lilac Gingham tag using the pattern. With a hole punch make hole in the tapered end of the tag. Cut a 6" piece of Lilac raffia and tie onto tag through punched hole. Glue tag onto the Lilac folding card. Gold emboss two small and one large butterfly stamps onto Strawberry Cream, Daffodil and Celery Solid papers. Cut out each butterfly leaving a small border around the stamped area. Glue to the tag with the large one in the middle and the smaller ones on either side as shown. Spread out Lilac raffia.

ANNOUNCEMENT

Base
Create a base size 4 ⅛" x 5 ⅝" from Grape Solid Mix 'n' Match Archivals paper. Cut a piece slightly smaller from Lilac Polkadots paper. Emboss swirly patterned stamp in gold on a section of Grape Polkadots paper. From that embossed section cut a small rectangle 3 ½" x 2 ¼". Center and glue the rectangle in the middle of the Grape and Lilac Polkadots layered card.

Butterflies
Emboss two small and one large butterfly stamps in gold onto Strawberry Cream, Daffodil and Celery Solid papers. Cut out each butterfly leaving a small border around the stamped area. Glue with the large butterfly in the middle and the smaller ones on either side as shown.

Create a folding card option for this project by mounting it on a 8 ½" x 5 ½" scored card stock.

Tip

Our Mix 'n' Match Raffia is a nice addition to any page. The colors coordinate with our paper colors and texture is another appealing element that you can use on your page. Our Raffia will lay flat and stay nice, even in a page protector.

May

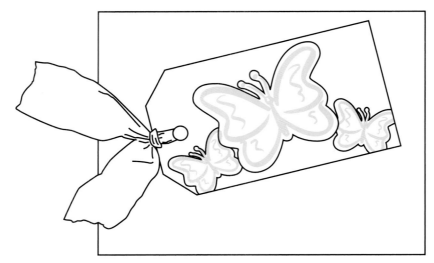

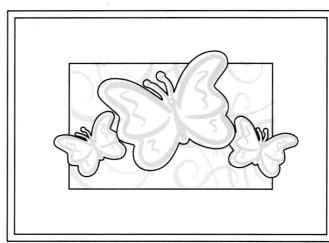

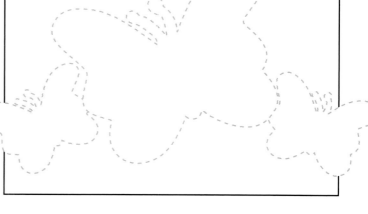

June

"THANK YOU"

Take time out
to create these
one-of-a-kind
Thank You cards.

MATERIALS CHECKLIST

PAPER:

☐ Hydrangea

☐ Mix 'n' Match Archivals
- Daffodil Solid
- Ivory Solid
- Lilac Solid
- Strawberry Cream Solid
- Wedgwood Solid

☐ Parchlucent
- Leaf

☐ Envelopes
- A-2 (4 ³/₈" x 5 ³/₄")
- A-7 (5 ¹/₄" x 7 ¹/₄")

TOOLS:

☐ Heat tool

☐ Punch Wheel
- Leaf

☐ Ruler

☐ Scissors, straight edge

☐ Scorer/Burnisher, natural bone

SUPPLIES:

☐ Archival Glue

☐ Embossing pad

☐ Embossing powder, gold

☐ Foam mounts

STAMPS: (from Hero Arts)

☐ "Dancing Flower" (A1492)

☐ "Thank You Set" (LL521)

☐ "Tic Tac Toe" (H1793)

HOW-TO INSTRUCTIONS

FOLDING CARD

Base
Start by making folding card from a sheet of 8 ½" x 11" Ivory Solid. Cut in half to 8 ½" x 5 ½". Then score with scorer/burnisher and fold in half to a folded size of 5 ½" x 4 ¼". Gold emboss tic tac toe grid and "Thank You" greeting onto Ivory folding card as shown.

Flowers
Gold emboss flower onto Daffodil, Lilac, Wedgwood and Strawberry Cream Solid Mix 'n' Match Archivals papers. Emboss two flowers in two colors of paper. Emboss three flowers in the remaining color. Cut out each leaving a small border around the stamped area. Choose a leaf style from the Leaf Punch Wheel and punch out leaf shapes from Leaf Parchlucent paper. Mount flowers on tic tac toe grid using foam mounts. Glue leaves coming out from under flowers.

ANNOUNCEMENT

Base
Create a base size 5 ⅛" x 6 ¾" from Hydrangea paper. Cut a 3 ½" x 5" rectangle from Ivory Solid and randomly gold emboss "Thank You"" greeting in a horizontal pattern leaving open areas for flowers to be placed. Center and glue Ivory rectangle on top of Hydrangea paper leaving approximately a ⅞" border.

Flowers
Gold emboss flowers onto Daffodil, Lilac, Wedgwood and Strawberry Cream Solid. Emboss two flowers in each color paper and cut out each leaving a small border around the stamped area. Choose a leaf style from the Leaf Punch Wheel and punch out leaf shapes from Leaf Parchlucent paper. Mount flowers between "Thank Yous" using foam mounts. Glue leaves coming out from under flowers.

Create a folding card option for this announcement by mounting it on a 8 ½" x 5 ½" scored card stock.

Tip

For punching in a specific spot with a Punch Wheel, turn the Punch Wheel over and use the round window as a guide for where you want to position your punched shape.

June
PATTERNS

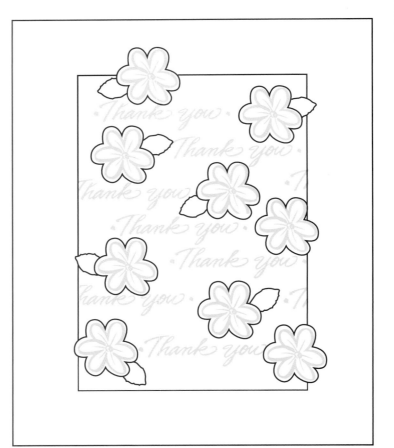

July

"INDEPENDENCE STAR"

USA

Mark the anniversary of our Nation's birth with these festive cards.

MATERIALS CHECKLIST

PAPER:

- ☐ Diamond Dust
  - Blueberry
  - Fire Engine Red
- ☐ Mix 'n' Match Archivals
  - Blueberry Polkadots
  - Blueberry Solid
  - Fire Engine Red Checkered
  - Fire Engine Red Solid
  - Sugar Solid
- ☐ Envelopes
  - A-2 (4 $^3/_8$" x 5 $^3/_4$")

TOOLS:

- ☐ Heat tool
- ☐ Punch Wheel
  - Classics
- ☐ Ruler
- ☐ Scissors, straight edge
- ☐ Scorer/Burnisher, natural bone

SUPPLIES:

- ☐ Archival Glue
- ☐ Dye ink pad, blue
- ☐ Embossing pad
- ☐ Embossing powder, gold
- ☐ Foam mounts
- ☐ Mix 'n' Match Raffia
  - Blueberry, pearlized
  - Fire Engine Red, pearlized
  - Sugar, pearlized

STAMPS: (from Hero Arts)

- ☐ "Alphabet and numbers" (LL478)
- ☐ "Fireworks" (G1470)
- ☐ "Star" (E1422)
- ☐ "Star" (E1424)
- ☐ "Star Set" (LL454)
- ☐ "Vintage Alphabet" (LL 405)

HOW-TO INSTRUCTIONS

FOLDING CARD I

Base Start by making a folding card from a sheet of 8 ½" x 11" Mix 'n' Match Archivals Blueberry Polkadots. Cut in half to 8 ½" x 5 ½". Then score with scorer/burnisher and fold in half to a folded size of 5 ½" x 4 ¼". Cut ½" thin red strip to fit across the width of the Blueberry Polkadots folding card and glue 1 ¼" from bottom on to folding card.

Stars Gold emboss large stars onto Fire Engine Red and Blueberry Diamond Dust papers. Cut around the stamped images leaving a tiny edge of color around the outside of the stamped image. Center and glue onto opposite color solid papers and trim again, leaving a tiny border. Stamp, cut and mount the same way with the smaller star stamp. For the two remaining stars, gold emboss onto Fire Engine Red and Blueberry Solid papers then cut leaving a paper border. Cut out a 1 ¼" x ⅞" rectangle from Fire Engine Red Checkered paper and stamp "USA" in blue then glue in the upper right corner of the folding card. Attach 3" strips of Fire Engine Red, Blueberry and Sugar pearlized raffia to the back of one large star. Mount all stars on folding card with foam mounts randomly as shown.

FOLDING CARD II

Base Start by making a folding card from a sheet of 8 ½" x 11" Fire Engine Red Diamond Dust. Cut in half to 8 ½" x 5 ½". With a burnisher score down the middle and then fold in half to a folded size of 5 ½" x 4 ¼" with the Diamond Dust to the inside and the white to the outside. Trim an ⅛" from the right side of the vertical front of the folding card only to allow a strip of Fire Engine Red Diamond Dust to show. Gold emboss fireworks on the front of the folding card.

Stars Gold emboss larger stars onto Fire Engine Red and Blueberry Diamond Dust papers. Cut around the stamped images leaving a tiny edge of color around the outside of the stamped image. Center and glue onto opposite color solid paper and trim again, leaving a tiny border. Attach strips of Fire Engine Red, Blueberry and Sugar pearlized raffia to two of the stars as pictured. Mount larger stars to folding card with foam mounts. Stamp "4th" in blue on white folding card in open areas around stars and fireworks. Using the Classics Punch Wheel punch out smaller stars from Fire Engine Red and Blueberry Diamond Dust papers and glue randomly over fireworks. To get outlined punched star, trim around a punched out star shape with a pair of tiny scissors.

Tip Not only can you decorate with punches but as in this project you can use the waste you normally throw away. Punch out your star and then cut out around the punched waste so you have another star in a larger size.

PATTERNS

(A)

(A)

(B)

(Place B here)

(Place A here)

(Place A here)

(B)

(Place B here)

August
"SUMMER VACATION"

Put some character into your summer greetings with these personalized cards.

MATERIALS CHECKLIST

PAPER:

- ☐ Country Charm Flowers
- ☐ Diamond Dust
  - Daffodil
- ☐ Mix 'n' Match Archivals
  - Celery Solid
  - Evergreen Solid
  - Grass Green Polkadots
  - Mocha Solid
  - Sugar Solid
- ☐ School Plaid
- ☐ Velveteen Paper
  - Daffodil
- ☐ Envelopes
  - A-2 (4 3/8" x 5 3/4")

TOOLS:

- ☐ Edge Accents Scissors
  - Deckle
- ☐ Punch Wheel
  - Classics

- ☐ Ruler
- ☐ Scissors, straight edge
- ☐ Scorer/Burnisher, natural bone

SUPPLIES:

- ☐ Archival Glue
- ☐ Colored Pencils
- ☐ Dye ink pad, black
- ☐ Foam mounts
- ☐ Markers
- ☐ Mix 'n' Match Raffia
  - Evergreen, pearlized
  - Lilac, pearlized

STAMPS: (from Hero Arts)

- ☐ "Cap" (C1331)
- ☐ "Football" (A1327)
- ☐ "Just Jessica" (K1730)
- ☐ "Just Michael" (K1731)

HOW-TO INSTRUCTIONS

FOLDING CARD I

Base   Start by making a folding card from a sheet of 8 ½" x 11" Country Charm paper. Cut in half to 8 ½" x 5 ½". Then score with scorer/burnisher and fold in half to a folded size of 5 ½" x 4 ¼". With a Deckle Edge Accents scissors cut a rectangle size 2 ⅞" x 4 ⅛" from Mix 'n' Match Archivals Celery Solid. Cut a second rectangle size 2 ⅝" x 3 ⅞" from Evergreen Solid. Layer Evergreen over Celery rectangle and glue, centered over Country Charm folding card.

Hula Girl   Stamp "Just Jessica" onto Sugar Solid paper with black ink. Add color with pencils. Cut a flower for her hair from Country Charm paper and glue in place. Create her top by stamping "Just Jessica" onto Daffodil Diamond Dust paper and trim top to fit. Cut out hula girl and glue centered on Evergreen Solid rectangle. Make her skirt from Evergreen pearlized raffia by slip knotting pieces of raffia onto one central strand of raffia. Make lei by tying successive knots in a piece of Lilac pearlized raffia then trim to correct size. Glue skirt and lei onto hula girl.

FOLDING CARD II

Base   Start by making a folding card from a sheet of 8 ½" x 11" School Plaid paper. Cut in half to 8 ½" x 5 ½". Then score with scorer/burnisher and fold in half to a folded size of 5 ½" x 4 ¼".

Football Player   Cut a Sugar rectangle size 2 ⅝" x 3 ⅞" and Stamp "Just Michael" in the center with black ink. Add color with pencils or markers. Stamp "Just Michael" again in black ink onto both Grass Green Polkadots Mix 'n' Match Archivals and Daffodil Velveteen Paper. Cut shirt from Grass Green Polkadots and pants from Daffodil. Stamp football onto Mocha Solid, and cap onto Daffodil Velveteen Paper. Cut out these accessory shapes right along the edges of the stamped images. Glue cap and pants in appropriate places. Mount football with foam mounts in players hand. Center and glue the Sugar rectangle with completed football player onto a rectangle size 2 ⅞" x 4 ⅛" of Daffodil Velveteen Paper. Center and glue layered piece onto School Plaid folding card. With Classic Punch Wheel punch stars from Evergreen Solid paper and glue at corners of layered piece as pictured.

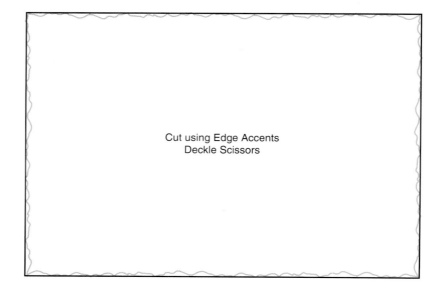

Cut using Edge Accents
Deckle Scissors

September

"BLOSSOMS"

Please join us
for a Bridal Shower
in honor of
Cindy Lai on
September 11 at
11:00 am
1530 Lake Grove SE
Grand Rapids, MI
R.S.V.P.

Randy & Gladys Bruwer
invite you to dinner
immediately following
the 8:00 p.m. wedding rehearsal of
Kristin Hosford and Josh Bruwer
Thursday, July 8th
at the Holiday Inn
Holland, Michigan

Regrets only – 458-7036

Watch your next gathering blossom with these beautiful invitations.

September

Please join us
for a Bridal Shower
in honor of
Cindy Lai on
September 11 at
11:00 am
1530 Lake Grove SE
Grand Rapids, MI
R.S.V.P.

Randy & Gladys Bruwer
invite you to dinner
immediately following
the 8:00 p.m. wedding rehearsal of
Kristin Hosford and Josh Bruwer
Thursday, July 8th
at the Holiday Inn
Holland, Michigan

Regrets only – 458-7036

MATERIALS CHECKLIST

PAPER:

- [ ] Diamond Dust
  - Lilac
- [ ] Mix 'n' Match Archivals
  - Celery Solid
  - Lilac Plaid
  - Lilac Polkadots
  - Lilac Solid
  - Sugar Solid
- [ ] Parchlucent
  - Crystal
- [ ] Envelopes
  - A-2 (4 $^3/_8$" x 5 $^3/_4$")
  - Square (6 $^1/_2$" x 6 $^1/_2$")

TOOLS:

- [ ] Heat tool
- [ ] Punch Wheel
  - Leaf

- [ ] Ruler
- [ ] Scissors, straight edge

SUPPLIES:

- [ ] Archival Glue
- [ ] Embossing pad
- [ ] Embossing powder, white
- [ ] Foam mounts
- [ ] Mix 'n' Match Raffia
  - Evergreen, pearlized
  - Lilac, pearlized
- [ ] Photo Corners, white

STAMPS: (from Hero Arts)

- [ ] "Flowers Border" (H1456)

HOW-TO INSTRUCTIONS

ANNOUNCEMENT

Invitation

Print invitation on Sugar Solid paper. Cut out printed copy creating a rectangle size 5" x 4 $^7/_8$". Glue Sugar Solid rectangle onto Lilac Diamond Dust rectangle size 5 $^5/_8$" x 4 $^1/_4$" and glue entire layered piece onto a base of Lilac Plaid size 5 $^7/_8$" X 4 $^5/_8$".

Flowers

White emboss three flowers onto Lilac Polkadot Mix 'n Match Archivals. Cut around the stamped images leaving a tiny edge of color around the outside of each stamped image. Arrange flowers to fit around pre-printed invitation on Sugar Solid and attach with foam mounts. Choose a leaf style from the Leaf Punch Wheel and punch out five leaf shapes from Celery Solid. Glue leaves under the edges of the flowers.

SQUARE ANNOUNCEMENT

Base

Cut Lilac Polkadots Mix 'n' Match Archivals paper into a 6 $^1/_4$" square. Cut smaller square of Lilac Solid paper size 5 $^1/_2$" square. Ink one flower in the border stamp and randomly stamp onto the Lilac Solid 5 $^1/_2$" square. Emboss in white.

Invitation

Imprint invitation message on a 8 $^1/_2$" x 11" sheet of Crystal Parchlucent paper with an inkjet or laser desktop printer. Cut pre-printed invitation to 5 $^1/_2$" square. Layer then center the Lilac and Parchlucent pieces on the Lilac Polkadots. Add white photo corners to secure all layers together. You may glue the Lilac solid to the Lilac Polkadots for security. Tie a Lilac raffia bow and glue in place as pictured.

Tip

With Mix 'n' Match Archivals it is easy to make coodinating pieces like wedding invitations, announcements, shower invitations, thank yous and reply cards - just pick the color and be creative.

(B)

(B)

(B)

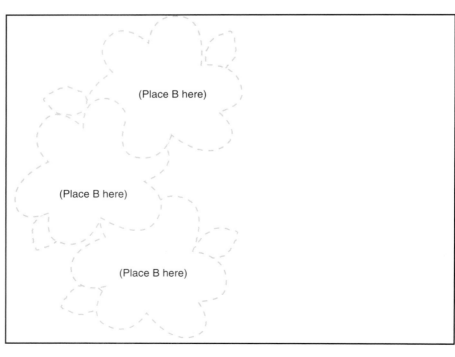

(Place B here)

(Place B here)

(Place B here)

October

"SPOOKTACULAR"

Make these spectacularly spooky cards for all the ghouls and goblins in your life.

MATERIALS CHECKLIST

PAPER:

- ☐ Big Boo
- ☐ Diamond Dust
  - Apricot
  - Daffodil
- ☐ Little Boo
- ☐ Mix 'n' Match Archivals
  - Apricot Polkadots
  - Apricot Solid
  - Licorice Polkadots
  - Licorice Solid
- ☐ Envelopes
  - A-2 (4 ³/₈" x 5 ³/₄")

TOOLS:

- ☐ Knife, craft/hobby
- ☐ Ruler
- ☐ Scissors, straight edge

SUPPLIES:

- ☐ Archival Glue
- ☐ Dye ink pad, black
- ☐ Foam Mounts
- ☐ Mix 'n' Match Raffia
  - Daffodil, pearlized

STAMPS: (from Hero Arts)

- ☐ "Happy Halloween" (F1170)
- ☐ "Pumpkin" (H276)

HOW-TO INSTRUCTIONS

FOLDING CARD I

Base

Start by making a folding card from a sheet of 8 ½" x 11" Licorice solid. Cut in half to 8 ½" x 5 ½". Then score with scorer/burnisher and fold in half to a folded size of 5 ½" x 4 ¼". Cut out a rectangle size 3" x 4 ¼" from Little Boo paper. Center and glue on top of a Apricot Polkadots rectangle size 4 ⅞" x 3 ½". Center and glue layered piece onto Licorice folding card.

Ghostly Greeting

Stamp "Happy Halloween" greeting in black onto Apricot Solid paper. Trim carefully around greeting leaving a slight border of Apricot. Glue greeting onto a piece of Daffodil Diamond Dust paper. Trim again leaving a border of the Daffodil Diamond Dust. Cut out a large ghost from the Big Boo paper. Mount diagonally with foam mounts onto the Little Boo paper part of the folding card. Punch little circles from Daffodil Diamond Dust for eyes and glue in place. With foam mounts, mount "Happy Halloween" greeting on top of ghost as shown.

FOLDING CARD II

Base

Start by making a folding card from a sheet of 8 ½" x 11" Apricot Diamond Dust paper . Cut in half to 8 ½" x 5 ½". Then score and fold in half to a folded size of 5 ½" x 4 ¼". Cut a 3 ¾" x 5" rectangle of Daffodil Diamond Dust and a 3 ½" x 4 ¾" rectangle of Licorice Polkadots and layer and center as pictured over Apricot Diamond Dust folding card. Glue all layers together.

Pumpkin

Stamp pumpkin on Apricot Diamond Dust Solid paper and cut out. Using a craft knife and using the stamped image as a guide cut out eye, nose and mouth areas and save for later use. Behind the pumpkin, glue a circle of Daffodil Diamond Dust paper cut slightly smaller than the pumpkin. Trim around the saved eye, nose and mouth pieces making them slightly smaller than their original openings. Center and glue back in place on top of the Daffodil Diamond Dust. Mount pumpkin with foam mounts onto the Licorice Polkadots rectangle. Cut a moon and star out of Little Boo paper and mount with foam mounts in the upper right corner as pictured. Cut about seven pieces of Daffodil pearlized raffia in slightly different lengths close to 4". Position raffia under pumpkin base and glue in place on Licorice Polkadot.

Tip

When gluing Diamond Dust to a porous sheet of paper all paper adhesives will work without fail, but we recommend these when adhering papers to Diamond Dust: Neutral pH Adhesive, Mounting Memories Keepsake Glue, Xyron adhesive, UHU Glue Stick, Sticky Dots, Zig 2-Way.

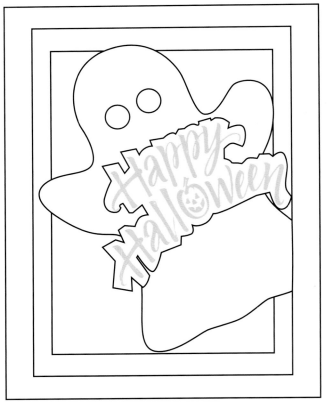

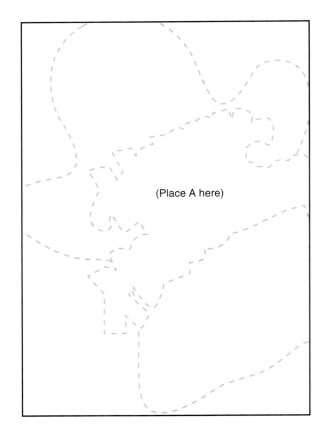

(Place A here)

(A)

November

"THANKSGIVING"

Happy Thanksgiving

Happy Thanksgiving

Show your
loved ones how
thankful you are
that they are part
of your life this year.

MATERIALS CHECKLIST

PAPER:

- ☐ Mix 'n' Match Archivals
  - Apricot Solid
  - Daffodil Solid
  - Fire Engine Red Solid
  - Mocha Plaid
  - Mocha Solid
- ☐ Mix 'n' Match Metallics
  - Gold Nugget
- ☐ Parchlucent
  - Terra
- ☐ Velveteen Paper
  - Mocha
- ☐ Envelopes
  - A-2 (4 ³/₈" x 5 ³/₄")
  - A-6 (4 ³/₄" x 6 ¹/₂")

TOOLS:

- ☐ Edge Accents Scissors
  - Deckle

- ☐ Heat tool
- ☐ Iron
- ☐ Punch Wheel
  - Leaf
- ☐ Ruler
- ☐ Scissors, straight edge
- ☐ Scorer/Burnisher, natural bone

SUPPLIES:

- ☐ Archival Glue
- ☐ Embossing pad
- ☐ Embossing powder, gold
- ☐ Foam mounts

STAMPS: (from Hero Arts)

- ☐ "Happy Thanksgiving" (F294)
- ☐ "Start Stampin' Leaves" (LL488)

HOW-TO INSTRUCTIONS

FOLDING CARD I

Base

Start by making a folding card from a sheet of 8 $\frac{1}{2}$" x 11" Mocha Plaid. Cut in half to 8 $\frac{1}{2}$" x 5 $\frac{1}{2}$". Then score with scorer/burnisher and fold in half to a folded size of 5 $\frac{1}{2}$" x 4 $\frac{1}{4}$". Use a warm iron to velvet emboss leaf stamps into a rectangular piece of Mocha Velveteen Paper size 3 $\frac{1}{2}$" x 5 $\frac{1}{4}$". Center and glue Mocha Velveteen Paper piece to a rectangle of Gold Nugget Solid paper size 3 $\frac{3}{4}$" x 5 $\frac{1}{2}$" or slightly smaller leaving a tiny gold border. Glue onto the face of the Mocha Plaid folding card.

Overlay

Gold emboss "Happy Thanksgiving" greeting onto Terra Parchlucent rectangle size 3 $\frac{5}{8}$" x 2 $\frac{1}{7}$". Center and attach the Terra Parchlucent overlay by gluing a Gold Nugget leaf punched with the Leaf Punch Wheel onto both the top of the Terra Parchlucent and Velveteen Papers.

FOLDING CARD II

Base

Start by making a folding card from a sheet of 8 $\frac{1}{2}$" x 11" Mocha solid. Cut in half to 8 $\frac{1}{2}$" x 5 $\frac{1}{2}$". Then score with scorer/burnisher and fold in half to a folded size of 5 $\frac{1}{2}$" x 4 $\frac{1}{4}$". With a Deckle Edge Accents scissors cut $\frac{5}{8}$" off the bottom edge of the face of the horizontal folding card. Create an Apricot Solid rectangle size 1" x 5 $\frac{1}{2}$". Deckle cut one of the 5 $\frac{1}{2}$" edges. Layer Apricot Solid piece on the face of the folding card from underneath to extend approximately $\frac{1}{4}$" beyond the Mocha deckled edge. Glue in place. In the same way create a strip of Gold Nugget Solid Mix 'n' Match Metallics and layer under the Apricot Solid deckled edge.

Greeting & Leaves

Gold emboss "Happy Thanksgiving" greeting onto lower right corner of the face of the Mocha folding card. Using the Leaf Punch Wheel punch out various leaves from Apricot Solid, Fire Engine Red Solid, Daffodil Solid and Gold Nugget Solid papers. Arrange in random fashion around the greeting and glue in place as pictured.

Tip

Velveteen Paper accepts heat embossing powder with great results. It's acid-free and can be used for scrapbooking. Velveteen Paper can also be used with most inkjet printers to print multicolor artwork or photos.

PATTERNS

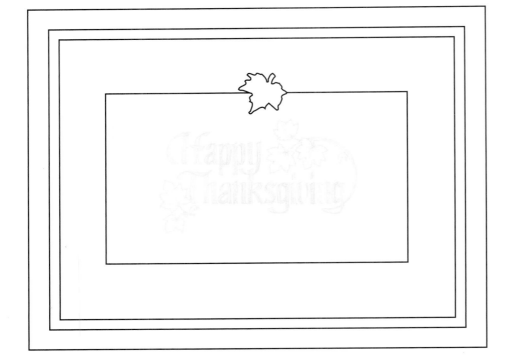

Cut bottom edge using Edge Accents Deckle Scissors

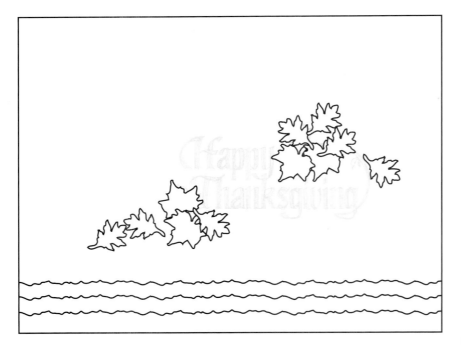

December
"BOUGHS OF HOLLY"

Send a Holiday card
that will stand out
from the rest.

MATERIALS CHECKLIST

PAPER:

- ☐ Mix 'n' Match Archivals
  - Fire Engine Red Polkadots
  - Fire Engine Red Solid
  - Grass Green Gingham
  - Grass Green Plaid
  - Grass Green Solid
- ☐ Envelopes
  - A-2 (4 3/8" x 5 3/4")

TOOLS:

- ☐ Heat tool
- ☐ Ruler
- ☐ Scissors, straight edge
- ☐ Scorer/Burnisher, natural bone

SUPPLIES:

- ☐ Archival Glue
- ☐ Embossing pad
- ☐ Embossing powder, gold
- ☐ Foam mounts
- ☐ Mix 'n' Match Raffia
  - Fire Engine Red, pearlized

STAMPS: (from Hero Arts)

- ☐ "Bold Holly" (F1796)

HOW-TO INSTRUCTIONS

FOLDING CARD I

Base
Start by making a folding card from a sheet of 8 ½" x 11" Fire Engine Red solid. Cut in half to 8 ½" x 5 ½". Then score with scorer/burnisher and fold in half to a folded size of 5 ½" x 4 ¼" . Cut a rectangle of Fire Engine Red Polkadots size 2 ¾" x 4 ⅛". Cut a rectangle from Fire Engine Red Polkadots paper 4 ⅛" x 2 ¾". Center and glue Polkadot paper onto a piece of Grass Green Gingham paper size 3 ⅜" x 4 ¾". Center and glue layered piece onto horizontal Fire Engine Red folding card.

Holly & Berries
Gold emboss holly only onto Grass Green Solid paper two times. Cut out around stamped holly leaves leaving a tiny border of Grass Green. Gold emboss berries only onto Fire Engine Red solid paper two times. Cut out around stamped berries leaving a tiny border of Fire Engine Red. Glue berries to holly. With foam mounts, mount holly with berries on top of the piece of Fire Engine Red Polkadots.

FOLDING CARD II

Base
Start by making a folding card from a sheet of 8 ½" x 11" Grass Green Gingham. Cut in half to 8 ½" x 5 ½". Then score with scorer/burnisher and fold in half to a folded size of 5 ½" x 4 ¼".

Present
Cut a rectangle size 3 ¼" x 3 ½" out of Fire Engine Red Solid. Stamp holly and berries all over Fire Engine Red rectangle in a random pattern and emboss in gold. Gold emboss holly only onto Grass Green Solid paper. Trim around stamped holy leaves leaving a tiny border of Grass Green. Gold emboss berries onto Fire Engine Red Solid paper. Cut out around stamped berries leaving a tiny border of Fire Engine Red. Glue berries to holly. Tie a piece of pearlized Fire Engine Red raffia around Fire Engine Red "box" and into a bow. With foam mounts, mount holly on top of the raffia below bow. Center and glue layered present onto Grass Green Plaid folding card.

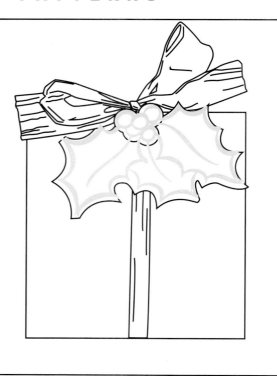

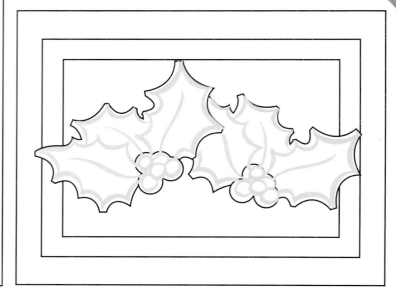

(A)

(A)

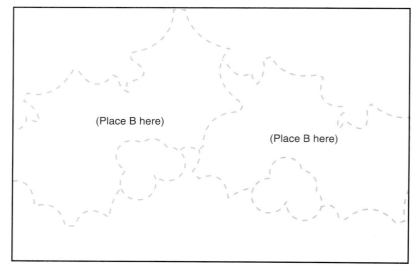

(Place B here)

(Place B here)

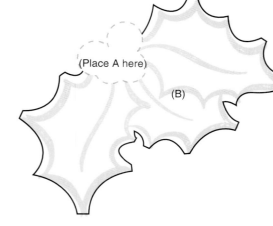

(Place A here)

(B)

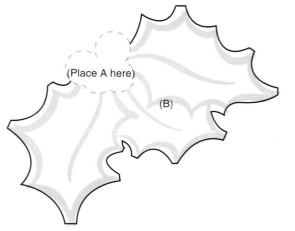

(Place A here)

(B)